THE

ECLIPSE

OF THE

RISING SUN

BOB UKOHA UKPABI

Copyright © 2020 by: BOB UKOHA UKPABI

ISBN: 9798593974990

Published in Nigeria by:

NKANEMI SERVICES

nkanemiservices@gmail.com

PROLOGUE

The Eclipse of the Rising Sun is about suffering and hardship we Africans pass through every day and their ugly consequences on psych of the people.

TABLE OF CONTENTS

1. CIRCUMSTANCES OF BIRTH (RANDY ROBERTS)

2. NIGERIA-BIAFRAN CIVIL WAR

3. EARLY EDUCATION

4. BANKING EXPERIENCE

5. DRUG ADDICTION AND ALCOHOLISM

6. FRUSTRATION AND SUICIDE ATTEMPT

7. REHABILITATION AND PARADIGM SHIFT

8. KICK-START A NEW CAREER IN BUSINESS CONSULTING

9. BUILT A BUSINESS EMPIRE AND MULTINATIONAL CONGLOMERATE

10. EPILOGUE

CHAPTER 1
ODYSSEY

Richard Roberts was born in 1930 to a very large polygamous family of four wives and many children. The name of the village is Etem South East Nigeria, the old Bende Division. It is a traditioanal community, ritualistic and where all pay allegiance to the Almighty-Obasi-Dineligwe. He was the first son from his mother with a sibling sister. **Unfortunately** his mother died very early and they were left orphans.

He did not have the opportunity to attend school except for the Sunday school organized by the Wesley Methodist Mission during those days of colonialism.

He was very gentle and obedient meek and mild child. He was sent to learn a trade at Calabar.

After a while his most elder brother was not satisfied with the treatment meted out to him, and therefore withdrew him for his own business. After the mandatory service on his brother's employment, he set up his own trade.

He dealt in "white immaculate shirts, starched and well ironed as was the vogue in those days in the 1950's 1960's". Their customers were the civil servants in government offices looking forward to taking over from the colonial over-Lords. Their trading post was the south-west region, opened along the axis of Ifo, Shagamu, Ijebu-Ode, Ibadan, Agege and Eko (Lagos). Business was good and the man was able to assist his family members and even sponsored some of his relatives to tertiary institution. This was the situation until the political disturbances in the south west which started about 1962 to 1966 coup-deta and later culminated into the Nigeria- Biafra war. The wild, wild west or "operation wetie", whereby opponents of AG/UPGA were doused with petrol which set a lot of people scampering to their home land and across the borders to the Cameroons. Awolowo was charged with treasonable felony and was sent to prison for 12 years. Chief Awolowo remained in opposition and vowed to make the region ungovernable.

It was about this time in 1962 that a son Randy was born to Mr. Roberts Richards. He was an itinerant trader, always travelling around the southern province, leaving his wife who was promiscuous all alone for months.

Being unable to comport and discipline her appetite for sex, she was painting the town red, sleeping around until she contracted sexually transmitted disease (STD) which she equally passed on to her unsuspecting husband on his return from the west. When Randy finally arrived, it reflected on his eyes, a squint, which made the man and the whole family to reject the child as a bastard according to beliefs and customs.

 However, the woman denied any wrong doing insisting her husband was responsible for her pregnancy. She said the man was responsible and that "only a woman knows the father of her children". Nevertheless no paternity test was conducted to verify the truth. After a long time the family conceded in order to forestall any stigmatization the incident would bring.

Mr. Richard Roberts continued in his business and he prospered and became very rich. But when in January, 1966, Nzeogwu and his misguided blood-thirsty army collogues carried out their revolution, totally unnecessary which eventually led to a retaliatory coup in July 1966 and a civil war which changed both the political and economic landscape of Nigeria and impoverished people like Mr Richard Roberts, who lost all sources of income as a result of that traumatic experience and could not get back to his feet until his demise in 2002. However other Igbo men had different stories to tell, because they were resilient, persistent, determined and confident. So they were able to reintegrate themselves back to the Federal United Nigeria, through the Government Policy of Reconstruction, Reconciliation and Rehabilitation.

CHAPTER 2
THE NIGERIA – BIABRA WAR

Chukwuemeka Odumegwu Ojukwu, the Oxford trained soldier, born of a millionaire father was appointed governor of the Eastern Region after the first coup of January 1966. However, after the retaliatory coup of July 1966 Ojukwu was mandated by Eastern Constituent Assembly (ECA) to declare an independent Republic of Biafra. This was because the Federal Republic of Nigeria could no longer guarantee the safety and security of life and property of Easterners in the North and all over Nigeria.

In that coup, the Head of State Major General Johnson Thomas, Umunnakwe

Aguiyi- Ironsi was killed by Northern soldiers led by Theophilus Danjuma, a christian from the Middle Belt and part of security details. Other soldiers of Eastern extraction as well as civilians numbering about 30,000 were murdered in the coup. The world press branded the killings a POGROM.

Biafra, was declared 30th May, 1967 and as a response the Nigerian military attacked. From the first shot fired at Gakem in Cross River in Biafra, a full-scale war broke out as Biafrans defended their mother land territory.

During the war after Aba was over-run in 1968, Mr. Roberts moved his family to the village, Etem. It was a traumatic experience as life was tough.

When the Hausa-Fulani Nigerian army invaded the village Etem, they colonized the community, appointing a Seriki to rule indirectly, just like the Lord Lugard era. They conscripted the women for sex, whether married or single, arrested all the chickens and domestic animals for food and oppressed the citizens. Note that in 1917 one of the villages in Etem Amaeke which earlier resisted Colonial invasion suffered a great massacre, just like the killings in Asaba. Therefore the people capitulated.

Between 1968 and 1970 they lived in the rain forest, living off berries, raw cassava and green vegetable. The situation was so bad that children were dying of a new plague, malnutrition (Kwasiokor) and lack of Medicare as Nigerian governments blockade would not allow essential commodities to be shipped into Biafra. It was really tough. people survived by the grace of God and prayers.

Women will leave their husbands and families to warm the beds of solders in exchange for food. While some gave information on the forward movement of the Biafra army, there was a lot of sabotage against the war effort of the Biafra high command. However Biafrans still defended their territorial intergrity.

The Biafra high command rejected the land corridor proffered by the Nigeria Government to bring food to people because they tried to poison the population to achieve extermination of Ndi-Igbo. Note, the American investigation confirmed it as some salt that came in through Ogwu corridor was mixed with cyanide when tested. As you recalled salt was a scarce commodity in Biafra throughout the period of aggression and mostly after Calabar and Uburu were lost by the Biafran armed forces which happened to be the only source of this vital commodity.

A woman was captured with her two-year-old son whom she thought would be a protection for her not to be taken away by soldiers. Notwithstanding the son, a Nigerian soldier took the mother and kept her against her will. In 1970 when the war was ended she already had three children for the soldier husband this is despite the code of conduct issued by the Yakubu Gowon Government as revealed in "My command" (Obasanjo, O.).

After the hostilities by January 1970 when a truce was reached and an amnesty negotiated, after Gen Ojukwu took a fight to Ivory Coast in search of peace.

The Easterners came out of the bush, malnourished, no food, no accommodation and no money.

Mr. Roberts had no support and could not even access the £20 offered by the Chief Obafemi Awolowo Finance Ministry as he had no bank account. He trekked to Nkporo the present day Ebonyi State while he was   supposed to go back to Aba to reclaim his apartment and start life over again.

When finally Mr. Roberts, was able to gather some money to relocate to Aba, the apartment he lived in before the war, was no longer available. The landlord waited and believing he will not return, moved his properties out and gave the room to a new tenant.   Roberts was stranded no money no accommodation the chances of his children going to school was remote, Indeed there was no plan especially for Randy for schooling at eight, therefore he was dispatched to go and stay with one of his friends while the other four were distributed, among members of the family. Randy was staying with his father's friend who also happened to be his godfather. AT that time in 1970, the man had a son. He was a widower and lived with a nephew. It was a pathetic situation for Randy, as the man's son Kancy, will go to school while he went to man the shop while he will be left alone in the yard playing all kinds of games. Randy was sent back to his parents when in the course of playing with other children, one of the kids got injured he was deported home. However, immediately after his mother sent him to the village to live with his grandmother to start schooling. That was how the journey to acquire western education started. He never liked school because of the discipline. He always liked the freedom to engage in things like, chasing grass-hopers and flying his kites.

CHAPTER 3
FORMAL EDUCATION

Randy was enrolled in Primary School in September, 1970 at Central School Amaokwe Etem ran by the Methodist Church circuit a dominant sect apart from the Roman Catholic in Ama-okwe his village. The school ran two campuses- the preparatory unit (Ota-akara) and the main school, Primary 1-6. It was a mission school controlled by the Church. However, the Board of education at Bende has a supervisory role over the institution.

Randy was already eight years old when he was admitted into the local Primary school but found it difficult to assimilate the lessons taught for lack of self confidence . He was shy and timid and could not read the "ABCD" alphabets or the vernacular "AB GB D E". With his slate embossed with black charcoal, most of the time he ended up in teacher Maduka's animal farm. He must go to the bush to cut grass for the pigs, and rabbits, which was the punishment for failing his reading test, which the teacher used as excuse to get him working on his farm. This ignoble situation persisted for a whole session. However, Randy passed his examination to be transferred to the main school but incidentally as a result of his lack of confidence, he refused to advance to the next class. He was afraid of academic requirement in the upper class.   When teacher Maduka was approached by his grandmother. He advised that since Randy had decided on his own accord to repeat the class, he should be allowed to do so. However this was a selfish advice as his motive was to continue having Randy as helper in his farm.

Nevertheless, repeating of elementary one paid-off as it helped to transform Randy to a brilliant and excellent pupil. From then henceforth he took between first and third positions in the class, most of the time, his name was always announced in the local church mission, in recognition of his excellent academic performance. Infact his brilliance culminated into his recording the best Common Entrance Examination result

(30 scores) in 1978 which earned him admission into one of the most prestigious colleges South East of Nigeria-Methodist College Uzuakoli.

Life in the village was very interesting. The cult activities, local customs and traditions, including the culture were unforgettable.   There was law and order and their execution were fair and just .
Those who stole, are tied up in the village square for seven days without food or water at the end of this incaseration the person is brought out, stripped naked and decorated with fresh palm leaves (omu) and then paraded round the village. After humiliating and parading, the person was released. Normally after such act, the "thief" leaves

the village   because he or she no longer had honor.

The other matter is   a woman who got pregnant out of wedlock. The girl will identify the man responsible and the community would gather all the rubbish in the village and heap them on their door-posts forming a mountain of rubbish dump. Such women   never marry from that village.

The moonlight play was always exciting and the children always looked forward to it. The one called ORORO (hide and seek game) was a source of immorality as   the young people always use it to engage in sexual activities   under the cover of darkness.

Randy was not admitted to any level of the cult in the village because her grandmother was a fellow of the Christian Women Fellowship, even though she could not read the Bible. However she had a very strong faith in Christ.

Randy was very notorious in the village because of his sexual escapades. He slept with many girls. He even shared the girls with his grandfather a Casanova. He later became the village "letter writer" or reader".

Randy hated farm work because he naturally had no energy. He was incapable of doing hard labour, trekking long distances or carrying heavy load on the head. Whenever school vacated he would do everything to proceed on holiday to Aba in the city.

Randy's grandma was a farmer while the husband traded in clothing materials (wrappers). The man being amorous, had Lovers all over the cities and grandma even encouraged him to bring them home. Randy never witnessed any quarrels or disagreements between the couple throughout his time in the village. The granny loved the children and had very large extended family and relatives. With such large family so to say there were always helpers at home and the farm.

Randy's sexual activities started when an aunt raped him at the age of eight. The aunt, who slept with little Randy on the same mat would massage Randy's penis and made him put his fingers in her vagina and sometimes the aunt would insert the boys erect penis in her vagina. Innocent and young, Randy did not know what that meant, but he engaged in it. This was a common practice in the village after hostilities of the civil war . In 1970 senior aunties who were not married molested young boys.

There were many negative influences in the village that affected Randy. He had an uncle who smoked heavily. The man smoked Benson and Hedges, Whenever he dropped the stub filter Randy would pick it up and inhale until he started smoking driedleaves, newspapers and cigarette. His other uncle always sent him to buy spirit and Cocoa-Cola, which were mixed and drank. Little wonder, Randy was involved in all these indulgences and vices. He was negatively influenced by seniors and environment which affected his character and conduct.

Randy had no good counselor or a mentor. He had no hero or any father figure to look up to. When he began to develop hairs on the face, armpit and private part at puberty, he became confused as he was ridiculed and taunted by peers. He became embarrassed and withdrawn, fearful and developed low- self esteem.

Randy was slow, laid back with low mental cognition. He lacked self management. He was always late to school and one of the teachers a very old man about 75 years, Mr. Lion Hart was always catching him coming to school late every day and to make him change the teacher always flogged him at the back which was painful. Randy hated this teacher.

The reason for Randy's lateness to school was his engagement in domestic chores in the morning like preparing breakfast with firewood which was slow at combustion, fetching of water and others.

After Elementary school Randy left the village for college in 1978 to attend the British Missionary institution called Methodist College in

Uzuakoli. At Methodist College his eyes were opened to a different world of learning. Randy was in the college for a year and half until when his brother who was sponsoring his education travelled to USA in search of the golden- fleece. He relocated to Aba and enrolled in a day school as the available resources could not sustain him in the boarding house. At Aba, he attended Wilcox Memorial Comprehensive Secondary School, Ogbor Hill. Randy joined the "hippies" who were doing drug called barbiturate (Chinese capsule). He never attended lectures. A science student who was always absent from the laboratory practicals. Randy's final result in 1983 was abysmal failure.

CHAPTER 4
CAREER IN BANKING

Having gotten a bad result in WAEC, without making the requisite grade for university admission, Randy roamed the streets of Aba for two and half years in search of white collar job. He did casual job with Dubic Breweries and subsidiary and other menial labor such as tailoring-"sewing panties", He later tried Disc Jockey (DJ) in one club or brothel, whereby music was played throughout the days in the week while a disco-party held on Sundays i.e. Sunday' Jams. Randy came in contact with harlots, criminals and people of questionable character. He drank alcohol and smoked cigarette.

In 1985, he was rescued by sister Cynthia, who had secured a job with an old generation financial institution called Dynamic Bank Nig Limited. Sister Cynthia was doing well in Lagos, brilliant and sharp.

Brought to Lagos by sister Cynthia in 1985. Randy was accommodated by a guy called Johnny who later introduced him to marijuana. Another level has started where all their foods were garnished with marijuana.

One day, as Johnny was standing at Masha bus-stop he saw Cynthia in a sports car with her boyfriend. He was mad and He wondered why Cynthia, who had well-off boyfriend kept Randy in his house. Not coming to terms with this, he made mockery of Randy.

That night Randy could not sleep and immediately reported the matter to Cynthia and decided he would go back to the East. When his uncle who lives in a big apartment and had turned his back on him heard about it , he went berserk with Randy and thundered "let that bastard go", if someone they trying to redeem from poverty and penury cannot be patient, "let him go". Jonny shifted ground and apologized to Randy saying he did not mean any harm. An office assistant job was secured for Randy eventually. Randy's short stay with

Johnny proved to be an ugly experience. He suffered insomnia and relied on sleeping pills, he encountered a man who asked why he was using the medicine and that man happened to be Eddie Okonta, the highlife musician who thrilled fans with his trumpet during the 60s. Other experiences were with women, harlots and crime. Arrangement was made on daily bases where Randy slept with the neighbors as the apartment was only a single room since he will always sleep over with his numerous women all night long.

Through one of Cynthia's acquaintances in the office, she succeeded in securing s job for Randy in the bank. Interestingly Randy had worked with a private company whose primary business objective was importation of commodities. After working with this organization for a while, Randy was transfered to represent the company in the Eastern zone with headquarters in Aba. Randy hated Aba because of his past experiences. Staff of the company he joined taught him how to steal from the company. The company was selling leather material imported from USA. The materials were measured according to the quantity demanded. What was done was buy one and take one at half the price.   Lack of integrity and collusion was the prime reaper. Randy made money fraudulently. There was a lot of money to enjoy pepper soup, drink and run around with women. Some of the boys turned their bed-room to nest of sex. Randy smoked marijuana recklessly and used other drugs. In 1987, Randy returned to Lagos, having secured another job with Dynamic Bank as a full clerical officer. That was how his banking career started, which he had to do for 28 years. He worked under stress and throughout these times he was most incompetent with very bad customer relation. He was always under pressure caused by his abuse of cannabis.

Randy's career in the industry was a monumental failure as he could not secure enough promotion to push him up the career ladder owing to incompetence. Randy shied away from leadership positions. He was stagnated or peaked in banking industry terms in the same position for several years until he eventually elected to voluntarily quit to avoiding being shipped out. He wasted all opportunities. He squandered the money he made on high lifestyle and never invested.

CHAPTER 5

SELF EDUCATION/ DRUG ADDICTION AND ALCOHOLISM

In 1990 Randy secured admission into University of Lagos (Unilag) COSIT Program. It was a BSc. Accounting correspondence programme in the faculty of Business Administration. Initially, he was performing excellently, with his experience in financial accounting acquired via GCE O level. At Ayilara, Ojuelegba, Lagos State he met Ruby who introduced him to the habit of using marijuana as a means of mental retention and a powerful means of "MEMORY RECALL". Infact, Ruby told him doctors and lawyers always use it, which account for their good performance in courts of law and hospitals.

Randy therefore increase his indulgence in the substance. Unfortunately for him he suffered withdrawal syndrome and could not come out it again.

In 1994 Randy experienced a psychedelic shock as a result of an over dose of marijuana . Diagnosis was Mannic-Melancholy and Affective Disorder. He was rescued but not completely rehabilitated. He lost his cognitive capacity and his mental competence.

He became a vegetable and frustration set in both in his career and education. Randy had a CGPA of 3.8 in 1990. By 2000 after 10 years in school for a degree course of 5 years by Unilag standard, his CGPA had declined to 1.8 and was only admitted to a Third Class in the Bachelor of Science degree, Randy was suffering internally, He sought one escape route or another and then went deeper into Marijuana, alcoholism and womanizing, which contributed to decimate and destroy his life. He could not invest and with the loss of his brain power, he could not put into practice all that he had learnt in school.

The genesis of Randy's precarious situation in life started early during childhood or teenage years. That was Randy's case. Early in life he was eating food laced with marijuana. He drank palm- wine, smoked cigarettes and was introduced to sex by an aunt who took advantage of his innocence.

CHAPTER SIX

FRUSTRATION AND SUICIDE

Randy was totally frustrated. He had a dysfunctional family and unable to sustain relationships. He found succor only in drugs and developed a constant death-wish. Most of the time he had insomnia i.e. unable to sleep, lack of appetite, and anxiety. Sometimes he could not go out because he had a feeling, that something bad, an accident could happen to him. His life was filled with constant fear. In fact Randy tried severally to take his life and if not for the entire family and the grace of God he would have committed suicide. Once he was invited to a birthday party where alcohol was not served. He left the party and started drinking from one beer parlour to another smoking cigarette. By the time the chips were down, he had drank as many as 12 bottles of big Stout and still craving for more bottles. Randy returned to the party to pick his family. Driving drunk, he lost control and his car had a head-on collision with an on-coming vehicle at Iyana-Isolo. Both vehicles badly damaged, but nobody died in the crash. Randy was saved just because he wore his seat-belt. His wife was also saved, just like the driver of the other vehicle.

Randy was to escape death in another drunk-driving accident. He rammed into a road divider at top speed, but survived. However, after that second crash Randy was traumatized, He was afraid of driving. The trauma left him destabilized. In 1994, Randy got a cable, "COME HOME GRANDMA DEAD" This was a great loss for him. So as he planned to go home for the funeral, having obtained some days off duty to travel to the village for a befitting burial of a virtuous woman. On the morning of his travel as he prepared, and packed his luggage. Suddenly he lost his mind that he forgot that he was to travel to the East. Confused he scattered everything in the house. From 6:00am to 6:00pm he was inside his room. Rigmarolling all-over the room. Sometimes he would lay down and masturbate. Another time he rolled on the ground and under the bed.

Randy will look at himself in the mirror and became alarmed. He disliked the image of himself that appeared. He hated himself and wanted to end it up immediately. He picked up the kitchen knife and placed it on his chest to piece the heart, but he lacked the courage to drive the knife through. So as he was trying while concentrating on the man in the mirror and continued to hate the image he was seeing with intensity as soon as he drew the knife for the last time. Cynthia banged on the door and Randy was startled. Filled with shock and anxiety, the knife fell off his grip. Cynthia continued to bang on the door.

 Eventually, when the door was opened and Cynthia saw the state of affairs with the room scattered and in disarray, she immediately raised alarm. When help came instead of taking him to a psychiatric facility, his relations just took him to a general practitioner who prescribed aspirin. Having been detained in a ward where his movement was restricted for days. He devised a strategy to escape from that prison and approached one of his radical dude called Tony Montana a medical consultant, who took him to one of their fraudulent hospital run by a Philipino, who has a medical- retainership with Dynamic Bank Plc. Randy was transferred to this medical facility, he was released without adequate treatment. On his release, Randy being cash strapped, he hit the road for the banks headquarters on Lagos Island. He boarded a bus without any money on him and when it was time to pay the bill, the conductor nearly threw him out of the bus. However, he was saved the embarrassment by a passenger, who paid. On getting to the banking hall, Tony was there who quickly escorted him away from that environment. He was supposed to be in hospital, not office. If management found out that he was not in hospital he would likely face Disciplinary Committee (DC) judgment to answer questions. He could loose his job. Besides any reasonable fellow would decipher from his unkempt and unstable mood and aggression that he was not okay.

 Randy exhibited psychosomatic behaviour. Things he stored in his sub-conscious mind 10-15 years ago,- hatred, resentment etc, were spilled out and resuscitated afresh.

He was diagnosed, with Manic-depression and later "Affective Disorder". He could not relax and adjust to the new state of mind brought about by the transition. He actually wanted to go back to the status quo (HIGH). His mind was heavy and the sedation he was intermittently administered weakened and made him drowsy. The state of his brain was pathetic as his cognitive ability was totally lost. He remained confused and destabilized. First he stopped the sedative by himself and later found succor in alcoholism and marijuana Due to withdrawal syndrome and the inability to adjust to the new transition government, Randy relapsed. He really needed a complete Rehab, detoxification and total reset of his brain and emotions before he could really be set free.

CHAPTER SEVEN

REHAB AND PARADIGM SHIFT

Randy's case was hopeless. This is because addiction is a demonic operation launched from the pit of hell by

the devil himself. This menace called addiction is

usually highly interconnected. You smoke marijuana, then you need cigarette to regain your sanity. Thereafter, the need for alcohol to log you down. Finally, when you stabilize you need a woman to caress your body.

All these are financial leakages. Even the production capacity is impaired as Randy was no longer able to carry out his conjugal activities.

With the effort of a lot of people and relatives and the mighty work that are being done by men of God in the Mountain of Fire Ministries Randy was saved and the yoke of Marijuana was finally broken. However, he was not completely free from alcohol and sometime cigarette smoking. This was an epoch and paradigm shift in Randy's life as he now a completely broken person and started a ministry for other miscreants who also have not found the courage to dump these bad habits that are destroying their lives and careers. With man it is not possible but with God all things are possible. The paradigm shift experience occurred when Randy was accosted by an angel in his dream who had pity on him and took away his reproach for life.

CHAPTER EIGHT
A NEW CAREER IN BUSINESS CONSULTING

Randy had to kick-start his new life. He conceptualized

 a new company called the Tree Concept Consulting (TTC) an outfit with a vision to becoming a leading consulting company on the African continent while his mission was providing financial services in strategic management, accounting services and industrial development in order to put African on the world map.

Most small businesses and start-ups are not ready to invest in training and financial education. But this happen to be fundamental for effective business development.

In Nigeria the education system never prepare individuals to becoming entrepreneurs but to seek for jobs which are not available. Given the exploding population at geometric progression while means of subsistence is increasing in arithmetic progression. Randy in his consulting firm would facilitate and train the citizens for effective performance while empowering them to grow the GDP of the economy for sustainable development. The people must participate and should be ready to bear the cost. Having realized that sustainable development cannot only he achieved by the multi-national enterprises but by the multiplicity of small businesses contributing humongous dividends to the national economy, It was only through this pragmatic means that United States of America(USA) was able to develop to her envious standard where most young Nigerians now want to migrate to take up menial jobs, which they cannot touch with a long spoon in their country. Even graduates are the culprits. However it behooves the government to build strong infrastructure and institutions that will be self-regulating and henceforth desist from the politics of North versus South dichotomy. A new value system of excellence, competency, truth, equity and justice should be installed in our community. We should no longer allow mediocrities to take charge of our leadership and economy. During the Biafran Nigerian War, the British government could not allow Biafras independence just because, the colonialist had constructed Nigeria as an economic unit, which when evaluated, has a very huge economic potentials. Even northern Nigeria, which was an economic leakage to the commonwealth office prior to the amalgamation by Lugard in 1914, now has huge deposit of mineral recourses within its topography.

Therefore, Nigeria, with an abundance mentality, will discover that there is enough for all and sundry. If the leadership will abandon the shameful looting of the treasury and nepotistic policy of appointing incompetent and mediocrities from the place of birth of leaders, things will improve. Nigerians are not lazy people. Even during the slave trade era, the British always preferred the Negro slave from the West Coast of Africa due to their strength and doggedness at work. We considered it that if the people are educated and trained in the right direction, ultimately the resources recovered from those foreign banks and deep wells where they are being laundered and stashed away in the North, South Europe and America, it is then and only then we can realize the true potentials of the Nigerian citizens and their leadership.

CHAPTER NINE
BUSINESS EMPIRE AND
MULTINATIONAL CONGLOMERATE

Randy from his consulting business, got together a group of intellectuals and excellent brains within Africa and abroad, to create a superstructure, producing house-hold goods, utilized by all and sundry in the society. The company sent economic mission abroad and attracted huge foreign investment (FDI). The foreign partners came down to Nigeria and established infrastructure and facilities to drive the economy.

The industries ranged from petrol-chemical, steel mills and automotive industry . With the in-road in the automotive industry, Nigeria was able to become independent of importation of used vehicles , which was almost making Nigeria a dumping ground for used, dilapidated and scrap vehicles. Infact if you observe closely some Nigerians in the street of London, Belgium, New York etc strolled the streets scavenging inside dump sites for condemned items which they eventually would ship to Nigeria and people rush to purchase them. This is the extent of the poverty level that the country is experiencing. Randy and company have been able to eradicate this menace.

He and his pace-setters have improved power supply due to improved infrastructures, to give the people better life. So let us look at the Big pictures. It is possible. It is do- able. No challenge is insurmountable, it is only the will and imagination that are needed to face any challenges and produce good result.

CHAPTER TEN
EPILOGUE

Randy so much resonate with the population that they called upon him to run for presidency, which he accepted. Forming his Consciousness and Transparency Party as a presidential candidate, he won by land slide. Randy, during his presidency, improved the lot of Nigerians, raised the per capital of the Nigerian people to $2000 per individual. His administration enthroned pragmatic governance, eradicated corruption, built strong institutions, and most of all developed the consciousness of the entire people to begin to think of what they can do for the country. Just like John F. Kennedy in the United States of

America said " Do not ask what your country can do for you but ask what can you do for your country". Patriotism was enthroned. People became more educated, happier and living longer. Randy was able to fulfill his destiny and leaving a LEGACY for all coming leaders to improve upon. Long Live Nigeria, Long Live the United, Indivisible, Republic of Nigeria.